MW00452995

Easy Cinnamon Cookbook

50 Delicious Cinnamon Recipes

By
BookSumo Press

Published by
http://www.booksumo.com

Table of Contents

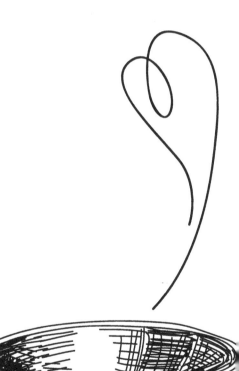

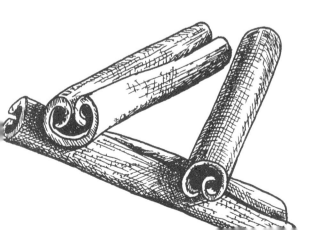
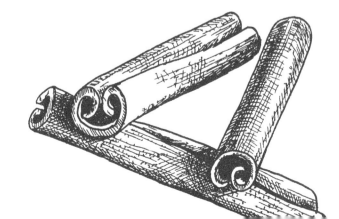

Simple
Cinnamon Syrup

🥣 Prep Time: 5 mins
🕐 Total Time: 25 mins

Servings per Recipe: 8
Calories	110 kcal
Fat	0 g
Carbohydrates	27.7g
Protein	0.2 g
Cholesterol	0 mg
Sodium	5 mg

Ingredients

1/2 C. white sugar
1/2 C. packed brown sugar
2 tbsp all-purpose flour
1/2 tsp ground cinnamon

1 tsp vanilla extract
1 C. water

Directions

1. In a pan, mix together the flour, brown sugar, white sugar and cinnamon.
2. Add the water and vanilla extract and stir to combine, then bring to a boil, stirring occasionally.
3. Boil, stirring occasionally till the mixture becomes thick like syrup.
4. Remove everything from the heat and keep aside to cool for about 10 minutes before serving.

EASIEST
Toast

Prep Time: 5 mins
Total Time: 7 mins

Servings per Recipe: 2
Calories   154 kcal
Fat   4.9 g
Carbohydrates   26.1g
Protein   2 g
Cholesterol   11 mg
Sodium   199 mg

Ingredients

2 slices white bread
2 tsp butter
2 tbsp white sugar

1 tsp ground cinnamon

Directions

1. In a toaster, toast the bread slices to desired toasting.
2. In a small bowl, mix together the sugar and cinnamon.
3. Place the butter over one side of each slices evenly.
4. Top each buttered side of the slice with the cinnamon mixture generously.

Old-Fashioned
Cinnamon Cake

Prep Time: 10 mins
Total Time: 30 mins

Servings per Recipe: 15
Calories	197 kcal
Fat	6.7 g
Carbohydrates	32g
Protein	2.8 g
Cholesterol	18 mg
Sodium	116 mg

Ingredients

1 C. white sugar
1/4 C. butter, cut into chunks
2 1/2 C. all-purpose flour
2 tsp baking powder
1 C. milk

1/4 C. butter, melted
2 tbsp brown sugar
1 pinch ground cinnamon

Directions

1. Set your oven to 350 degrees F before doing anything else.
2. In a bowl, add the butter chunks and sugar and with a spoon, mix well.
3. Add the flour and baking powder and mix well.
4. Gradually, add the milk, stirring continuously till well combined.
5. Transfer the mixture into a 13x9-inch baking dish evenly and top with the melted butter, brown sugar, and cinnamon.
6. Cook everything in the oven for about 20-25 minutes.

CLASSIC
Cinnamon Croutons

🥣 Prep Time: 5 mins

🕐 Total Time: 25 mins

Servings per Recipe: 4

Calories	141 kcal
Fat	6.6 g
Carbohydrates	18.8g
Protein	2 g
Cholesterol	15 mg
Sodium	211 mg

Ingredients

2 tbsp softened butter
4 slices white bread
2 tbsp cinnamon sugar

Directions

1. Set your oven to 375 degrees F before doing anything else.
2. Place the butter over both sides of each slices evenly, then cut the slices into cubes.
3. In a large bowl, place the slice cubes and sprinkle with the cinnamon sugar.
4. In a baking sheet, place the bread cubes in a single layer and cook everything in the oven for about 20 minutes, stirring once in the middle way.

Traditional
Christmas Cookies

🥣 Prep Time: 20 mins
🕐 Total Time: 1 hr

Servings per Recipe: 24
Calories   79 kcal
Fat   4.3 g
Carbohydrates   9.5g
Protein   0.7 g
Cholesterol   1 mg
Sodium   28 mg

Ingredients

1/4 C. white sugar
1 sheet frozen puff pastry, thawed
1 tbsp butter, melted
1/3 C. white sugar
3/4 tsp ground cinnamon

1/8 tsp ground cardamom
water

Directions

1. Set your oven to 375 degrees F before doing anything else and line a baking sheet with parchment paper.
2. Spread 1/4 C. of the sugar over a smooth surface.
3. Unfold the puff pastry over sugar and roll out to a 15x10-inch rectangle.
4. In a bowl, mix together the remaining sugar, cinnamon and cardamom.
5. Coat the pastry with the melted butter evenly and top with the cinnamon mixture evenly.
6. Starting from the long edge of the pastry, roll pastry tightly around filling, stopping in the middle.
7. Repeat with the opposite edge, meeting the first roll.
8. With your wet fingers press gently so the two rolled edges stay together.
9. Refrigerate for about 5-10 minutes.
10. Cut the pastry into 1/4-inch slices and place onto prepared baking sheet in a single layer about 1-inch apart.
11. Cook everything in the oven for about 12 minutes.

DIVINE
Apples

Prep Time: 5 mins
Total Time: 7 mins

Servings per Recipe: 4
Calories	41 kcal
Fat	0.1 g
Carbohydrates	10.8g
Protein	0.2 g
Cholesterol	0 mg
Sodium	1 mg

Ingredients

2 apples, diced
1 tsp white sugar
1/2 tsp ground cinnamon

Directions

1. In a microwave safe bowl, place the apples and microwave for about 30 seconds.
2. Now, sprinkle the apples with the cinnamon and sugar and microwave for about 1 minute.

Gooey
Biscuits

Prep Time: 15 mins
Total Time: 30 mins

Servings per Recipe: 8
Calories	560 kcal
Fat	27.7 g
Carbohydrates	86.3g
Protein	8.7 g
Cholesterol	19 mg
Sodium	609 mg

Ingredients

1 1/4 C. Reduced Fat Bisquick
1 C. whole wheat baking mix
2/3 C. buttermilk
2 C. Cinnamon Chips
1 C. cinnamon coated raisins

3 tbsp melted butter
1/2 C. confectioners' sugar
1 tbsp melted butter
1 tbsp water

Directions

1. Set your oven to 425 degrees F before doing anything else.
2. In a food processor, add the cinnamon chips and pulse till grounded roughly.
3. Transfer half of the roughly grounded chips into a bowl and pulse the remaining chips till grounded finely.
4. Add baking mixes and rains in the bowl with the roughly grounded cinnamon chips and mix.
5. In the center of the mixture, make a well and slowly, add the buttermilk and mix till a dough forms.
6. Place the dough onto a floured surface and knead for about 1 minute.
7. Flat the dough into a 10x8-inch rectangle shape and coat with 3 tbsp of the melted butter evenly.
8. Place the finely grounded cinnamon chips on top evenly. Starting from the long edge of the pastry, roll pastry tightly. With your wet fingers press gently so the two rolled edges stay together.
9. Cut the pastry into 8 equal slices and place onto a baking sheet in a single layer about 1-inch apart.
10. Cook everything in the oven for about 12 minutes.
11. Meanwhile in a bowl, mix together the remaining ingredients and drizzle over the biscuits.

MOUTH WATERING
Bacon

Prep Time: 10 mins
Total Time: 20 mins

Servings per Recipe: 8
Calories   297 kcal
Fat   8 g
Carbohydrates   54.4g
Protein   7.7 g
Cholesterol   20 mg
Sodium   432 mg

Ingredients

1 1/2 C. ground cinnamon
1 1/2 C. white sugar
1 lb. maple-smoked turkey bacon

Directions

1. In a bowl, mix together the sugar and cinnamon and coat the bacon with the mixture evenly.
2. Heat a large skillet on medium-low heat.
3. Add the bacon and cook for about 6-8 minutes, flipping occasionally.
4. Transfer the bacon onto a paper towel lined plate to drain.

Yummiest
Crisp

Prep Time: 5 mins
Total Time: 45 mins

Servings per Recipe: 8
Calories	394 kcal
Fat	13.1 g
Carbohydrates	64.5g
Protein	5.2 g
Cholesterol	15 mg
Sodium	328 mg

Ingredients

1/4 C. butter
1 (10 oz.) package miniature marshmallows
9 C. crispy rice cereal
2 tbsp ground cinnamon
1 C. slivered almonds

1/4 C. raisins

Directions

1. Grease an 8x8-inch baking dish and keep aside.
2. In a large pan, mix together the marshmallows and butter on medium heat and melt, stirring continuously.
3. Remove everything from the heat and immediately, stir in the remaining ingredients.
4. Transfer the mixture into the prepared baking dish evenly and press gently to smooth the surface.
5. Refrigerate for about 30 minutes and then cut into desired sized squares.

DELICIOUS
Rice Pudding

Prep Time: 5 mins
Total Time: 30 mins

Servings per Recipe: 4
Calories	243 kcal
Fat	2.3 g
Carbohydrates	51g
Protein	4.4 g
Cholesterol	1 mg
Sodium	28 mg

Ingredients

1 C. uncooked rice
2 C. water
2 tbsp nonfat milk
5 tbsp raisins
2 tsp margarine

1/2 tsp ground cinnamon
1 tsp sugar

Directions

1. In a pan mix together the rice, raisins, margarine, milk and water on medium-high heat and bring to a boil, stirring occasionally.
2. Reduce the heat to low and simmer, covered for about 15 minutes.
3. In a bowl, mix together the sugar and cinnamon.
4. Sprinkle the sugar mixture over the rice mixture and serve.

American
Christmas Cookies

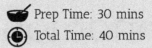 Prep Time: 30 mins
Total Time: 40 mins

Servings per Recipe: 48
Calories	55 kcal
Fat	2.3 g
Carbohydrates	8.1g
Protein	0.8 g
Cholesterol	9 mg
Sodium	20 mg

Ingredients

1/2 C. butter, softened
3/4 C. packed brown sugar
1 tsp ground cinnamon
1/4 tsp baking powder
1 egg
1 tsp vanilla extract
2 C. all-purpose flour

1 tbsp superfine sugar
1/2 tsp cinnamon
1 egg white, beaten
3 tbsp mini chocolate chips

Directions

1. Set your oven to 375 degrees F before doing anything else and grease cookie sheets.
2. In a bowl, add the brown sugar and butter and beat till creamy.
3. Add the egg, baking powder, 1 tsp of the cinnamon and vanilla and mix well.
4. Slowly, add the flour, mixing till a stiff dough forms. Take about 1 tbsp of the dough and roll into 6-inch long ropes.
5. Curl up one end of the rope slightly to make the head, then curl the rest of the rope towards the head in a spiral shape to make the snail shell.
6. Repeat with the remaining dough. Arrange onto prepared cookie sheets in a single layer about 2-inches apart.Coat the cookies with the egg whites.
7. In a small bowl, mix together the superfine sugar and remaining cinnamon. Sprinkle the cinnamon mixture over cookies evenly. With chocolate chips, make eyes on the heads.
8. Cook everything in the oven for about 8 minutes.

HOLIDAY SPECIAL
Cinnamon Pinwheels

Prep Time: 25 mins
Total Time: 50 mins

Servings per Recipe: 12
Calories	238 kcal
Fat	17.5 g
Carbohydrates	18.7g
Protein	2.1 g
Cholesterol	45 mg
Sodium	114 mg

Ingredients

1 C. butter
1 1/2 C. all-purpose flour
1/2 C. sour cream
3 tbsp white sugar
1 tsp ground cinnamon

3 tbsp white sugar
1 tbsp water

Directions

1. In a bowl, add the flour and with a pastry cutter, cut the butter.
2. Add the sour cream and mix well.
3. Refrigerate, covered for at least 8 hours.
4. In a small bowl, mix together the cinnamon and 3 tbsp of the sugar.
5. Divide the dough into 2 portions.
6. Sprinkle the floured smooth surface with some sugar.
7. Roll both the portions in 20x7-inch rectangles and sprinkle with the cinnamon mixture.
8. Roll each rectangle tightly, beginning on the 7-inch side and pinch the sides to seal.
9. Wrap and refrigerate at least 1 hour but no longer than 48 hours.
10. Set your oven to 350 degrees F.
11. Cut each roll into 1/4-inch slices and place onto a cookie sheet in a single layer about 2-inch apart.
12. In a bowl, mix together the water and remaining sugar.
13. Coat the cookies with the sugar mixture evenly.
14. Cook everything in the oven for about 20-25 minutes.

North European
Pastries

Prep Time: 30 mins
Total Time: 1 hr 55 mins

Servings per Recipe: 18
Calories	227 kcal
Fat	13.1 g
Carbohydrates	25.1g
Protein	3.1 g
Cholesterol	45 mg
Sodium	262 mg

Ingredients

1 (8 oz.) package cream cheese
1 C. white sugar, divided
1 egg yolk
3 tbsp ground cinnamon
18 slices bread, crust removed

3/4 C. butter, melted

Directions

1. In a bowl, add the cream cheese, egg yolk and 14 C. of the sugar and beat till smooth.
2. In a shallow dish, place the melted butter.
3. In another shallow dish, mix together the cinnamon and remaining sugar.
4. Spread cream cheese mixture over 1 side of each bread slice.
5. Roll each bread slice in jelly roll style.
6. Dip each roll into beaten egg and then roll into cinnamon mixture.
7. In a baking dish, place the rolls and freeze, covered for at least 1 hour.
8. Set your oven to 350 degrees F before doing anything else.
9. Cook everything in the oven for about 25 minutes.

TRADITIONAL
French Cookies

Prep Time: 20 mins
Total Time: 40 mins

Servings per Recipe: 6
Calories   434 kcal
Fat   24.9 g
Carbohydrates   49.6g
Protein   4.5 g
Cholesterol   123 mg
Sodium   187 mg

Ingredients

2 eggs
1 C. white sugar
1 C. all-purpose flour
1/8 tsp ground nutmeg
3/4 C. butter, melted and cooled

1/2 tsp almond extract
1/2 tsp ground cinnamon

Directions

1. Set your oven to 350 degrees F before doing anything else and grease madeleine molds.
2. In a double broiler, add the sugar and eggs and heat, beating continuously.
3. Remove everything from the heat and keep aside to cool.
4. Add the remaining ingredients and mix till well combined.
5. Transfer the mixture into prepared madeleine molds.
6. Cook everything in the oven for about 15 minutes.
7. Serve with a sprinkling of the powdered sugar.

Old-Time
Cookies

Prep Time: 15 mins

Total Time: 25 mins

Servings per Recipe: 60

Calories	95 kcal
Fat	3.4 g
Carbohydrates	15.1g
Protein	1.3 g
Cholesterol	15 mg
Sodium	90 mg

Ingredients

4 C. sifted all-purpose flour
1 tsp baking soda
1 tsp salt
1 C. butter
2 C. white sugar
2 eggs

2 tsp vanilla extract
1 1/2 C. buttermilk
1/2 C. white sugar
2 tsp ground cinnamon

Directions

1. In a bowl, sift together the flour, baking soda and salt and keep aside.
2. In a bowl, add the sugar and sugar and beat till creamy.
3. Add the eggs, one at a time beating continuously.
4. Add the buttermilk and vanilla and stir to combine.
5. Slowly, add the flour mixture, mixing trill well combined.
6. Refrigerate, covered for overnight.
7. Set your oven to 400 degrees F and grease cookie sheets.
8. With a rounded spoon, place the mixture onto the prepared cookie sheets in a single layer about 2-inch apart.
9. In a small bowl, mix together the white sugar and cinnamon.
10. Cook everything in the oven for about 8-10 minutes.

SOFT
Cinnamon Pretzels

Prep Time: 30 mins
Total Time: 40 mins

Servings per Recipe: 24

Calories	257 kcal
Fat	8.4 g
Carbohydrates	42.7 g
Protein	4.2 g
Cholesterol	22 mg
Sodium	169 mg

Ingredients

2 C. milk
1/2 C. honey
6 C. all-purpose flour
2 tsp baking soda
1/2 C. white sugar

1/2 C. ground cinnamon
1 C. butter, melted
1/2 C. white sugar
1/2 C. ground cinnamon

Directions

1. Set your oven to 400 degrees F before doing anything else and grease 2 cookie sheets.
2. In a bowl, mix together the honey and milk and keep aside for about 5 minutes.
3. In a large bowl, sift together the flour and baking soda.
4. Add the milk mixture and mix till a soft dough forms.
5. Place the dough onto a lightly floured surface and knead for about 3 minutes.
6. With a rolling pin, roll the dough into a 1/2-inch thick rectangle and then cut into 24 equal parts.
7. Roll each piece into 10-inch cylinder and then fold the ends together into a pretzel-shape.
8. In a bowl, mix together 1/2 C. of the cinnamon and 1/2 C. of the sugar.
9. Top the pretzels with the cinnamon mixture evenly.
10. Place the pretzels on the prepared baking sheet and cook everything in the oven for about 8 minutes.
11. In a bowl, mix together the melted butter, 1/2 C. of the cinnamon and 1/2 C. of the sugar.
12. Coat the warm pretzels with the butter mixture.

Nutty
Cookie Bars

Prep Time: 20 mins
Total Time: 50 mins

Servings per Recipe: 24
Calories   190 kcal
Fat   12.8 g
Carbohydrates   17.7g
Protein   2.5 g
Cholesterol   28 mg
Sodium   155 mg

Ingredients

1 C. butter, softened
1 C. white sugar
1 egg, whites and yolks separated
2 C. all-purpose flour
1 1/2 tbsp ground cinnamon

1 tsp salt
1 1/2 C. chopped walnuts

Directions

1. Set your oven to 325 degrees F before doing anything else and grease and flour a 16x11-inch baking dish.
2. In a bowl, sift together the flour, cinnamon and sat.
3. In another bowl add the sugar and butter and beat till creamy.
4. Add the flour mixture and egg yolks and mix till well combined.
5. Transfer the mixture into prepared baking dish.
6. In a small bowl, add the egg whites and beat till foamy.
7. Coat the top of the flour mixture with the beaten egg white and top with the walnuts.
8. Cook everything in the oven for about 30 minutes.

FAMILY FAVORITE
Corn Casserole

🥣 Prep Time: 5 mins
🕐 Total Time: 1 hr 5 mins

Servings per Recipe: 5	
Calories	481 kcal
Fat	22.1 g
Carbohydrates	70.3g
Protein	7.6 g
Cholesterol	10 mg
Sodium	747 mg

Ingredients

1/2 C. margarine
1/2 C. white sugar
1/4 C. all-purpose flour
2/3 C. evaporated milk
2 (15 oz.) cans whole kernel corn, drained

1/4 C. white sugar
1 tsp ground cinnamon

Directions

1. Set your oven to 350 degrees F before doing anything else and lightly grease and flour a casserole dish.
2. In a pan, add 1/2 C. of the sugar and margarine and heat till margarine melts completely.
3. Add the flour and stir to combine and immediately, remove everything from the heat.
4. Add the evaporated milk and beat well.
5. Stir in the corns and transfer the mixture into prepared casserole dish.
6. Cook everything in the oven for about 1 hour.
7. Serve with a topping of the 1/4 C. of the sugar and cinnamon.

Moist
Tea Time Cake

Prep Time: 20 mins
Total Time: 40 mins

Servings per Recipe: 8
Calories   244 kcal
Fat   11.9 g
Carbohydrates   33.5g
Protein   2.1 g
Cholesterol   31 mg
Sodium   285 mg

Ingredients

7 tbsp butter, melted
1 C. self-rising flour
1/2 C. white sugar
1 tbsp ground cinnamon
1/3 C. milk
1 tbsp white sugar

1/2 tsp ground cinnamon
1 tbsp butter
1/4 C. white sugar
1 1/2 tsp ground cinnamon

Directions

1. Set your oven to 350 degrees F before doing anything else and lightly grease a 6-inch round cake pan.
2. In a bowl, add the self-rising flour, 1/2 C. of the sugar, melted butter and 1 tbsp of the cinnamon and mix till a soft dough forms.
3. Add the milk and mix till smooth.
4. Transfer the mixture into prepared cake pan.
5. Cook everything in the oven for about 15-20 minutes.
6. Remove everything from the oven and keep aside to cool completely.
7. In a pan, melt the remaining butter.
8. Add the 1/2 tsp of the cinnamon and 1 tbsp of the butter and stir to combine.
9. Spread the butter mixture over the cake evenly.
10. In a small bowl mix together the remaining 1/4 C. of the sugar and 1 1/2 tsp cinnamon.
11. Serve the cake with a sprinkling of the cinnamon mixture.

NORTH AMERICAN
Rolls

Prep Time: 15 mins
Total Time: 45 mins

Servings per Recipe: 12
Calories	198 kcal
Fat	6.7 g
Carbohydrates	32g
Protein	3.1 g
Cholesterol	27 mg
Sodium	545 mg

Ingredients

1/4 C. chilled butter, cubed into 1/4-inch size
2 1/2 C. baking mix
1/2 C. milk
1 egg
2 tbsp margarine, softened

3 tbsp white sugar
1 1/2 tsp ground cinnamon
1 C. confectioners' sugar
1 tbsp milk

Directions

1. Set your oven to 425 degrees F before doing anything else and grease an 8-inch square pan.
2. In a bowl, add the flour and cubed butter and toss to coat well.
3. In another bowl, add the egg and 1/2 C of the milk and beat well. Add the egg mixture into the flour mixture and mix till a dough formed.
4. Place a clean cloth over a board and dust with the flour generously. Place the dough floured cloth and knead for about 10 times.
5. Roll the dough into a 15x8-inch rectangle and cat with the margarine.
6. In a small bowl, mix together the cinnamon and sugar and spread over the dough.
7. Roll the dough tightly, starting from the 15-inch side and pinch the edges.
8. With a sharp knife, cut into 12 slices and arrange into the prepared pan, cut side down.
9. Cook everything in the oven for about 15 minutes.
10. Remove everything from the oven and keep aside to cool.
11. In a bowl, mix together the confectioners' sugar and 1 tbsp of the milk.
12. Drizzle over the buns and serve.

German Star Cookies

🥣 Prep Time: 20 mins
🕐 Total Time: 40 mins

Servings per Recipe: 18
Calories   190 kcal
Fat   10.7 g
Carbohydrates   21.2g
Protein   5 g
Cholesterol   0 mg
Sodium   24 mg

Ingredients

2 2/3 C. finely ground almonds
1 tbsp ground cinnamon
1 tsp lemon zest
1/3 C. egg whites
1/8 tsp salt

2 1/2 C. confectioners' sugar
1 3/4 tsp lemon juice

Directions

1. Set your oven to 325 degrees F before doing anything else and line the cookie sheets with the parchment papers.
2. In a bowl, mix together the almonds, lemon zest and cinnamon.
3. In another bowl, add the egg whites and salt and beat till soft peaks form.
4. Gradually, sift the confectioner's sugar, beating continuously till stiff peaks form.
5. Reserve about 1/3 C. of the mixture.
6. Sprinkle confectioner's sugar onto a smooth surface.
7. Place the dough onto smooth surface and roll into 14-inch thickness.
8. With a star shaped cookie cutter, cut the cookies.
9. Arrange the cookies onto prepared cookie sheets.
10. For glaze, add the lemon juice in reserved almond mixture and stir till smooth.
11. Coat the tops of the cookies with the glaze and cook everything in the oven for about 20-25 minutes.

CINNAMON
Pepper Chicken

Prep Time: 10 mins
Total Time: 40 mins

Servings per Recipe: 4
Calories	143 kcal
Fat	1.7 g
Carbohydrates	3g
Protein	27.7 g
Cholesterol	68 mg
Sodium	1822 mg

Ingredients

4 skinless, boneless chicken breast halves
1 tsp ground cinnamon
2 tbsp Italian-style seasoning
1 1/2 tsp garlic powder
3 tsp salt

1 tsp ground black pepper

Directions

1. Set your oven to 350 degrees F before doing anything else and grease a 13x9-inch baking dish.
2. In the bottom of the prepared baking dish, place the chicken breasts.
3. Sprinkle with the remaining ingredients and cook everything in the oven for about 30 minutes.

Holiday Favorite
Pie

Prep Time: 20 mins
Total Time: 35 mins

Servings per Recipe: 8
Calories	302 kcal
Fat	13.6 g
Carbohydrates	41.2g
Protein	4.2 g
Cholesterol	35 mg
Sodium	192 mg

Ingredients

1 C. white sugar
1 1/2 tbsp all-purpose flour
1 tsp ground cinnamon
1 pinch salt
1 egg, beaten

2 tbsp butter, melted
1 tsp vanilla extract
1 1/2 C. milk
1 (10 inch) unbaked pie crust

Directions

1. Set your oven to 400 degrees F before doing anything else.
2. In a large bowl, mix together the flour, sugar, cinnamon and salt.
3. Add the butter, egg, milk and vanilla and beat till well combined.
4. Transfer the mixture into a 10-inch unbaked pie crust.
5. Arrange the pie crust in a glass pie plate and cook everything in the oven for about 15 minutes.
6. Now, set the oven to 350 degrees F and cook everything in the oven for about 45 minutes.

GOURMET
Cinnamon Rolls

🥣 Prep Time: 2 hrs

🕐 Total Time: 2 hrs 20 mins

Servings per Recipe: 16

Calories	372 kcal
Fat	19 g
Carbohydrates	45.2g
Protein	6.4 g
Cholesterol	51 mg
Sodium	198 mg

Ingredients

1/4 C. water at room temperature
1/4 C. butter, melted
1/2 (3.4 oz.) package instant vanilla pudding mix
1 C. warm milk
1 egg, room temperature
1 tbsp white sugar
1/2 tsp salt
4 C. bread flour
1 (.25 oz.) package active dry yeast
1/2 C. butter, softened
1 C. brown sugar
4 tsp ground cinnamon
3/4 C. chopped pecans
1 (4 oz.) package cream cheese, softened
1/4 C. butter, softened
1 C. confectioners' sugar
1/2 tsp vanilla extract
1 1/2 tsp milk

Directions

1. In a bread machine pan, place the water, 1/4 C. of the melted butter, vanilla pudding, 1 C. of the warm milk, egg, 1 tbsp of the sugar, salt, bread flour, and yeast

2. Select the dough cycle and press the start. When cycle completes, remove the dough from the machine. Place the dough onto floured surface and roll to 17x10-inch rectangle. In a bowl, mix together the cinnamon, brown sugar and pecans.

3. Coat the dough with the about 1/2 C. of the melted butter evenly and top with the cinnamon mixture. From the longer side, cut into 16 one-inch slices and arrange onto a greased 13x9-inch baking dish.

4. Keep aside in warm place for about 45 minutes. Set your oven to 350 degrees. Cook everything in the oven for about 15-20 minutes. Remove everything from the oven and keep aside to cool till just warm.

5. Meanwhile in a bowl, mix together the remaining ingredients. Top the warm buns with the cream cheese mixture and serve.

Incredible
Coffee Cake

Prep Time: 30 mins
Total Time: 1 hr 10 mins

Servings per Recipe: 24

Calories	282 kcal
Fat	15.7 g
Carbohydrates	34.1g
Protein	2.8 g
Cholesterol	31 mg
Sodium	275 mg

Ingredients

1 (18.25 oz.) package yellow cake mix
1 (3.4 oz.) package instant vanilla pudding mix
1 (3.4 oz.) package instant butterscotch pudding mix
4 eggs
1 C. water

1 C. vegetable oil
1 C. packed brown sugar
1 tbsp ground cinnamon
1 C. chopped walnuts

Directions

1. Set your oven to 350 degrees F before doing anything else and grease a 10-inch bundt cake pan.
2. In a large bowl, mix together the butterscotch pudding mix, vanilla pudding mix and cake mix.
3. Add the oil, eggs and water and mix till well combined.
4. In another bowl, mix together the remaining ingredients.
5. Place half of the cake mix mixture in the bottom of the prepared cake pan and top with the half of the cinnamon mixture
6. Repeat the layers once and cook everything in the oven for about 20 minutes.
7. Now, set the oven to 325 degrees F and cook everything in the oven for about 35-40 minutes.

PROTEIN-PACKED
Almond Snack

🥣 Prep Time: 15 mins

🕐 Total Time: 1 hr 15 mins

Servings per Recipe: 16

Calories	231 kcal
Fat	18 g
Carbohydrates	13.3g
Protein	7.8 g
Cholesterol	0 mg
Sodium	40 mg

Ingredients

1 egg white
1 tsp cold water
4 C. whole almonds
1/2 C. white sugar
1/4 tsp salt

1/2 tsp ground cinnamon

Directions

1. Set your oven to 250 degrees F before doing anything else and grease a 10x15-inch jellyroll pan.
2. In a bowl, add the egg whites and beat well.
3. Add the water and beat till frothy.
4. Add the almonds and mix till well combined.
5. Add the remaining ingredients and stir to combine.
6. Transfer the mixture into the prepared jellyroll pan and cook everything in the oven for about 1 hour.

Summertime
cool Treat

Prep Time: 5 mins
Total Time: 1 hr 50 mins

Servings per Recipe: 8
Calories	279 kcal
Fat	17.5 g
Carbohydrates	28.4g
Protein	3.5 g
Cholesterol	104 mg
Sodium	48 mg

Ingredients

1 C. white sugar
1 1/2 C. half-and-half cream
2 eggs, beaten
1 C. heavy cream
1 tsp vanilla extract

2 tsp ground cinnamon

Directions

1. In a pan, mix together the half-and-half and sugar on medium-low heat.
2. Bring to a simmer and immediately remove everything from the heat.
3. In a pan, beat the eggs.
4. Add half of the sugar mixture and immediately, beat till well combined.
5. Return the egg mixture into the pan with heavy cream and stir to combine.
6. Place the pan on medium-low heat and cook, stirring continuously till the mixture thickens.
7. Remove everything from the heat and immediately, stir in the cinnamon and vanilla.
8. Keep aside to cool completely.
9. Transfer the mixture into an ice cream maker and process according to manufacturer's directions.

HEARTY
Bread

🥣 Prep Time: 30 mins
🕐 Total Time: 3 hrs 20 mins

Servings per Recipe: 36
Calories	182 kcal
Fat	4.1 g
Carbohydrates	32.4g
Protein	4.1 g
Cholesterol	18 mg
Sodium	115 mg

Ingredients

1 1/2 C. milk
1 C. warm water (110 degrees F/45 degrees C)
2 (.25 oz.) packages active dry yeast
3 eggs
1/2 C. white sugar
1 tsp salt
1/2 C. margarine, softened

1 C. raisins
8 C. all-purpose flour
2 tbsp milk
3/4 C. white sugar
2 tbsp ground cinnamon
2 tbsp butter, melted

Directions

1. In a pan, add the milk and heat till it bubbles.
2. Remove everything from the heat and keep aside to cool till lukewarm.
3. In a bowl, dissolve the yeast in warm water and keep aside till frothy.
4. Add the margarine, sugar, eggs, raisins ans salt and mix till well combined.
5. Add the milk and stir to combine.
6. Slowly, add the flour, mixing till a stiff dough forms.
7. Place the dough onto a lightly floured surface and knead for a few minutes.
8. In a large greased bowl, place the dough and turn till the dough coats completely.
9. With a damp cloth, cover the dough and keep aside till doubles.
10. Grease a 9x5-inch loaf pans.
11. Place the dough onto a floured surface and roll to 1/2-inch thick rectangle.
12. Coat the dough rectangle with 2 tbsp of the milk.

13. Roll the dough tightly about 3-inches in diameter.
14. Cut the dough into thirds, and tuck under ends.
15. Place the loaves into prepared loaf pans and coat the tops with some butter, then keep aside for about 1 hour.
16. Set your oven to 350 degrees F.
17. Cook everything in the oven for about 45 minutes.
18. Remove the loaves from the pans and coat with the melted butter before serving.

AMERICAN STYLE
Waffles

🥣 Prep Time: 10 mins
🕐 Total Time: 25 mins

Servings per Recipe: 3
Calories	380 kcal
Fat	19.4 g
Carbohydrates	39.3g
Protein	11.4 g
Cholesterol	181 mg
Sodium	821 mg

Ingredients

2 egg yolks
1 tsp vanilla extract
1 C. buttermilk
1/4 C. butter, melted
1 C. all-purpose flour
1 1/2 tsp baking powder
1/2 tsp baking soda

1/2 tbsp white sugar
1/4 tsp salt
2 egg whites
1 pinch ground cinnamon

Directions

1. Set you waffle iron to heat before doing anything else.
2. In a bowl, add the butter, buttermilk, eggs and vanilla and beat well.
3. In a third bowl, add the egg whites and beat till stiff.
4. In another bowl, mix together the remaining ingredients.
5. Add the flour mixture into the egg mixture and mix till well combined, then fold in the egg whites.
6. Place the desired amount of the mixture and cook till golden brown.

Wonderful
Frosting

🍲 Prep Time: 10 mins

🕐 Total Time: 20 mins

Servings per Recipe: 16	
Calories	146 kcal
Fat	5.9 g
Carbohydrates	23.8g
Protein	0.2 g
Cholesterol	16 mg
Sodium	67 mg

Ingredients

1 tsp instant coffee granules
1/2 tsp ground cinnamon
1 pinch salt
1 tsp vanilla extract
1/2 C. butter, softened

3 C. confectioners' sugar
1/3 C. milk

Directions

1. In a bowl, add the instant coffee and with the back of the spoon, mash till powdered.
2. Add the salt and cinnamon and stir to combine.
3. In another bowl, add the butter and beat till smooth.
4. Add the cinnamon mixture and vanilla and stir to combine.
5. Add the confectioners' sugar and milk and beat till desired consistency.

CHRISTMAS
Snack

Prep Time: 5 mins

Total Time: 10 mins

Servings per Recipe: 3

Calories	121 kcal
Fat	8.3 g
Carbohydrates	9.9g
Protein	4.5 g
Cholesterol	0 mg
Sodium	93 mg

Ingredients

1 large stalk celery, cut into 3 pieces
3 tbsp peanut butter
1 tsp ground cinnamon

2 tbsp raisins

Directions

1. Arrange the celery pieces on a clean surface, hollow part facing up.
2. Sprinkle with the cinnamon evenly.
3. Place the peanut butter into the hollow and top with the raisins.

Easy
Breakfast Granola

🥣 Prep Time: 10 mins
🕐 Total Time: 2 hrs 20 mins

Servings per Recipe: 12
Calories	295 kcal
Fat	11 g
Carbohydrates	44.6 g
Protein	5.8 g
Cholesterol	14 mg
Sodium	43 mg

Ingredients

1 1/4 tbsp olive oil
5 C. rolled oats
1 tbsp ground cinnamon
1/3 C. butter
1/4 C. honey
1 tbsp molasses

1/2 C. packed brown sugar
1/2 C. blanched slivered almonds
1/2 C. dried cherries

Directions

1. In a large pan, heat the oil on medium heat and cook the oats and cinnamon for about 3-4 minutes, stirring continuously.
2. Transfer the oats into a large bowl.
3. In the same pan, add the butter and heat till melted.
4. Add the molasses, brown sugar and honey and bring to a gentle simmer, then immediately, stir in the oats.
5. Cook till the oats heated through.
6. Remove everything from the heat and stir in the cherries and almonds.
7. Transfer the mixture onto a large cookie sheet and keep aside to cool.
8. Transfer the granola into an airtight container and store at room temperature.

SWEET
Flavorful Butter

🥄 Prep Time: 10 mins

🕐 Total Time: 20 mins

Servings per Recipe: 12

Calories	85 kcal
Fat	7.7 g
Carbohydrates	4.5g
Protein	0.1 g
Cholesterol	20 mg
Sodium	56 mg

Ingredients

1/2 C. butter, softened
1/4 C. dark brown sugar
1/4 tsp ground cinnamon

Directions

1. In a bowl add all the ingredients and beat till creamy and smooth.

Crunchy
Snack

Prep Time: 10 mins
Total Time: 30 mins

Servings per Recipe: 36
Calories	82 kcal
Fat	2.8 g
Carbohydrates	13.2g
Protein	1.2 g
Cholesterol	0 mg
Sodium	65 mg

Ingredients

1 C. white sugar
1 tsp ground cinnamon
1/4 tsp ground nutmeg

10 (8 inch) flour tortillas
3 C. oil for frying

Directions

1. In a resealable plastic bag, mix together the sugar, cinnamon and nutmeg and toss to coat.
2. In a large deep skillet, heat the oil to 375 degrees F and fry the tortilla chips in batches for about 30 seconds per side,
3. Transfer the tortilla chips onto a paper towel lined plate to drain.
4. Place the warm chips in the bag and shake to coat well.
5. Store in an airtight container.

DELIGHTFUL
Cheesecake

Prep Time: 10 mins
Total Time: 40 mins

Servings per Recipe: 12
Calories	483 kcal
Fat	30.7 g
Carbohydrates	44.9 g
Protein	6.3 g
Cholesterol	61 mg
Sodium	532 mg

Ingredients

2 (10 oz.) cans refrigerated crescent dinner rolls
2 (8 oz.) packages cream cheese, softened
1 C. white sugar
1 tbsp vanilla extract
1/2 C. butter, melted

1/2 C. white sugar
1 tbsp ground cinnamon

Directions

1. Set your oven to 350 degrees F before doing anything else.
2. Flatten one tube of the crescent roll dough and place into the bottom of a 13x9-inch baking dish and press it.
3. In a bowl, add the 1 C. of the sugar, cream cheese and vanilla and mix till smooth.
4. Place the cream cheese mixture over the dough evenly.
5. Unroll the remaining crescent roll dough and arrange over the top of the cream cheese layer.
6. Place the melted butter on the top evenly and sprinkle with the mixture of 1/2 C. of the sugar and cinnamon.
7. Cook everything in the oven for about 30 minutes.
8. Remove everything from the oven and keep aside to cool completely.
9. Refrigerate before serving.

Healthy
Fruity Rice

Prep Time: 10 mins
Total Time: 30 mins

Servings per Recipe: 4

Calories	240 kcal
Fat	0.5 g
Carbohydrates	56.3g
Protein	3.5 g
Cholesterol	0 mg
Sodium	153 mg

Ingredients

3/4 C. uncooked white rice
1 1/2 C. apple juice
1 apple, cored and chopped
1/3 C. raisins
1/2 tsp ground cinnamon

1/4 tsp salt, or to taste
1/4 C. chopped fresh parsley

Directions

1. In a pan, mix together the rice, raisins, chopped apple, apple juice, cinnamon and salt and bring to a boil.
2. Reduce the heat to low and simmer, covered for about 17 minutes.
3. Stir in the fresh parsley and serve immediately.

CHRISTMAS TREE
Ornaments

🥣 Prep Time: 10 mins
🕐 Total Time: 20 mins

Servings per Recipe: 15
Calories	76 kcal
Fat	0.3 g
Carbohydrates	23.3g
Protein	1 g
Cholesterol	0 mg
Sodium	3 mg

Ingredients

3 C. applesauce
3 C. ground cinnamon

Directions

1. In a bowl, add the cinnamon and applesauce and mix till a thick mixture forms.
2. Place the mixture onto a smooth surface and flatten it, then cut into cookie cutter shape.
3. Arrange the cookie shapes onto a cookie sheet and dry for about 3-4 days.

Classic
Rice Pudding

Prep Time: 10 mins
Total Time: 55 mins

Servings per Recipe: 12

Calories	436 kcal
Fat	17.8 g
Carbohydrates	58.7g
Protein	11.7 g
Cholesterol	119 mg
Sodium	159 mg

Ingredients

3 quarts milk
2 tbsp ground cinnamon
1/4 C. butter
2 C. white sugar
1 C. heavy cream

4 eggs
1 C. uncooked white rice

Directions

1. In a large pan, mix together the milk, rice, butter and cinnamon and bring to a boil.
2. Reduce the heat to low and simmer for about 30 minutes.
3. Slowly, stir in the sugar.
4. In a bowl, add the eggs and heavy cream and beat till smooth.
5. Slowly, add 1 C. of the hot milk mixture, mixing continuously.
6. Now slowly, add the eggs mixture into the pan, mixing continuously.
7. Reduce the heat to low and simmer, stirring continuously for about 10 minutes.
8. Transfer the mixture into a large serving bowl and keep aside to cool.
9. Refrigerate to chill before serving.

SPRINGTIME
Sugar Snap Peas

Prep Time: 5 mins
Total Time: 9 mins

Servings per Recipe: 2
Calories	81 kcal
Fat	2.4 g
Carbohydrates	11.1g
Protein	2.8 g
Cholesterol	0 mg
Sodium	160 mg

Ingredients

1 (8 oz.) package sugar snap peas
1 tsp olive oil
sea salt and freshly ground black pepper to taste

1/2 tsp ground cinnamon
1/2 tsp white sugar

Directions

1. Set the oven to broiler and arrange oven rack about 6-inches from heating element.
2. In a bowl, add the sugar snap peas and olive oil and toss to coat well.
3. In a baking sheet, place the sugar snap peas in a single layer.
4. In a small bowl, mix together the remaining ingredients.
5. Top the sugar snap peas with the cinnamon mixture evenly and cook under broiler for about 4-5 minutes.

Weeknight
Carrots

Prep Time: 15 mins
Total Time: 40 mins

Servings per Recipe: 8
Calories	169 kcal
Fat	6 g
Carbohydrates	29.2g
Protein	1.2 g
Cholesterol	15 mg
Sodium	122 mg

Ingredients

2 lb. carrots, peeled and sliced
1/4 C. butter, melted
1/4 C. orange juice
1/3 C. brown sugar

1/3 C. white sugar
1 tsp ground cinnamon

Directions

1. Set your oven to 350 degrees F before doing anything else.
2. In a pan of salted water, add the carrots and bring to a boil.
3. Reduce heat to medium-low and simmer for about 5 minutes, then drain well.
4. In a bowl, add the butter, white sugar, brown sugar, cinnamon and orange juice and beat till the sugars dissolve completely
5. Add the carrots and toss to combine well.
6. Transfer the carrots with the glaze to a baking dish and cook everything in the oven for about 15-20 minutes.

THANKSGIVING
Sweet Potatoes

🥘 Prep Time: 5 mins
🕐 Total Time: 8 hrs 15 mins

Servings per Recipe: 6
Calories	230 kcal
Fat	9.2 g
Carbohydrates	35.5g
Protein	2.4 g
Cholesterol	0 mg
Sodium	375 mg

Ingredients

1/4 C. vegetable oil
2 lb. sweet potatoes, peeled and sliced
2 tbsp brown sugar
1 tsp ground cinnamon
3/4 tsp salt

1 pinch freshly ground pepper
1 tbsp fresh lime juice

Directions

1. Set your oven to 375 degrees F before doing anything else.
2. In a 13x9-inch baking dish, add the oil and place in the oven for about 5 minutes.
3. Arrange the potatoes over the hot oil and cook everything in the oven for about 20 minutes, flipping once in the middle way.
4. In a small bowl, mix together the cinnamon, brown sugar, salt, and black pepper.
5. Cook everything in the oven for another 10 minutes.
6. Transfer the potatoes onto a paper towel lined plate to drain.
7. Serve with a drizzling of the lime juice.

Beet
Pickles

Prep Time: 10 mins
Total Time: 55 mins

Servings per Recipe: 16
Calories	91 kcal
Fat	0.1 g
Carbohydrates	23g
Protein	0.5 g
Cholesterol	0 mg
Sodium	103 mg

Ingredients

2 (15 oz.) cans sliced beets, drained with liquid reserved
3/4 C. distilled white vinegar

1 1/2 C. white sugar
2 (3 inch) cinnamon sticks

Directions

1. In a pan, add the cinnamon sticks, sugar, vinegar and reserved beet liquid on medium-high heat.
2. Bring to a boil and cook, stirring continuously till the sugar dissolves completely.
3. Reduce the heat to medium-low and simmer for about 5 minutes.
4. Place the mixture over the sliced beets and stir to combine.
5. Refrigerate, covered for at least 8 hours before serving.

CLASSIC
Crepes

🥣 Prep Time: 30 mins

🕐 Total Time: 2 hrs

Servings per Recipe: 8
Calories   361 kcal
Fat   14.8 g
Carbohydrates   50.4g
Protein   7.9 g
Cholesterol   75 mg
Sodium   127 mg

Ingredients

3 eggs
1/4 tsp salt
2 C. all-purpose flour
2 C. milk
1/4 C. vegetable oil
1/2 tsp ground cinnamon
4 Granny Smith apples, peeled and diced
1/2 C. white sugar

2 tsp cinnamon
2 tbsp water
2 tbsp cornstarch
1 tbsp water
1 1/2 tbsp milk
8 tsp vegetable oil, divided

Directions

1. In a bowl, add the eggs and salt and beat well.
2. Slowly, add the flour, stirring continuously.
3. Add 2 C. of the milk and mix till well combined.
4. Add 1/4 C. of the vegetable oil and 1/2 tsp of the cinnamon and mix well.
5. Refrigerate the mixture for at least 1 hour.
6. In a pan, Mix together the apples 2 tsp of the cinnamon, sugar and 2 tbsp water on medium heat.
7. In a small bowl, add the cornstarch and 1 tbsp of the water and beat well.
8. Add the cornstarch mixture in the pan and simmer for about 8-10 minutes, stirring occasionally.
9. Remove everything from the heat and keep aside, covered to keep warm.
10. Remove the flour mixture from the refrigerator and stir in the remaining milk.
11. In a crepe pan, heat 1 tsp of the oil on medium heat.

12. Add about 1/3 C. of the mixture and rotate the pan to cover the bottom of pan completely.
13. Cook for about 1 minute, flipping once in the middle way.
14. Repeat with the remaining oil and mixture.
15. Place the apple mixture in each crepe evenly and fold around the filling and serve.

CHEWY
Cookies

Prep Time: 20 mins
Total Time: 45 mins

Servings per Recipe: 36
Calories	177 kcal
Fat	8.6 g
Carbohydrates	24g
Protein	2.4 g
Cholesterol	24 mg
Sodium	94 mg

Ingredients

1 C. butter
2 C. white sugar
2 eggs
1 tsp vanilla extract
1 tbsp molasses
2 C. all-purpose flour
1 1/2 tsp baking soda

1 tsp ground cinnamon
1 C. chopped walnuts
2 C. quick cooking oats
1/2 C. semisweet chocolate chips
2/3 C. raisins

Directions

1. Set your oven to 350 degrees F before doing anything else and grease cookie sheets.
2. In a bowl, add the sugar and butter and beat till creamy.
3. Add the molasses, eggs and vanilla and beat till well combined.
4. In another bowl, mix together the flour, baking soda and cinnamon.
5. Slowly, add the flour mixture into the butter mixture, mixing till well combined.
6. Fold in the chocolate chips, raisins and oatmeal.
7. With a tsp, place the mixture onto prepared cookie sheets in a single layer and cook everything in the oven for about 12 minutes.

Hungarian Style
Bread

🥣 Prep Time: 15 mins

🕐 Total Time: 45 mins

Servings per Recipe: 20
Calories	215 kcal
Fat	9.7 g
Carbohydrates	28.3g
Protein	5.1 g
Cholesterol	27 mg
Sodium	210 mg

Ingredients

1 C. milk, room temperature

1 egg, beaten

2 tbsp butter, softened

1 1/2 tsp salt

3 tbsp white sugar

3 C. bread flour

2 tsp bread machine yeast

FILLING:

3 tbsp butter, melted

2/3 C. brown sugar

3/4 tsp ground cinnamon

1 C. chopped walnuts

1 C. raisins

TOPPING:

1 egg, beaten

1 tbsp water

1/2 C. chopped walnuts

Directions

1. In a bread machine pan, place the 1 egg, salt, 3 tbsp of the sugar, flour and yeast.

2. Select the dough cycle and press the start.

3. When cycle completes, remove the dough from the machine.

4. Punch down the dough and keep aside for about 5 minutes.

5. Place the dough onto floured surface and roll to 24x10-inch rectangle.

6. Coat the dough with the melted butter evenly and top with the cinnamon, brown sugar, raisins and 1 C. of the walnuts.

7. From the longer side, roll tightly in a jelly roll style.

8. Arrange onto a prepared baking sheet and shape it into a ring by sealing the ends.

9. Keep aside in warm place for about 1 hour.
10. Set your oven to 375 degrees F before doing anything else.
11. In a small bowl, add 1 tbsp of the water and 1 egg and beat well.
12. Coat the dough with the egg mixture evenly and top with the remaining walnuts.
13. Cook everything in the oven for about 20 - 25 minutes.
14. If the ring becomes browns too quickly, just cover with foil and continue to bake.

Aromatic
Granola

Prep Time: 10 mins
Total Time: 1 hr 10 mins

Servings per Recipe: 16
Calories	213 kcal
Fat	8.7 g
Carbohydrates	30g
Protein	5 g
Cholesterol	0 mg
Sodium	2 mg

Ingredients

3 C. old-fashioned oats
2 C. quick oats
1 C. chopped pecans
1/2 C. toasted wheat germ
1/4 C. maple syrup
2 tbsp Corn Oil

2 tbsp pure vanilla extract
4 tsp ground Saigon cinnamon
1/2 tsp ground nutmeg
1 C. dried cranberries

Directions

1. Set your oven to 300 degrees F before doing anything else and grease a baking sheet.
2. In a large bowl, mix together the quick oats, old-fashioned oats, wheat germ and pecans.
3. In another bowl, mix together the remaining ingredients except the cranberries.
4. Place the mixture over the oats mixture and stir to combine.
5. Transfer the mixture into the prepared baking sheet evenly and cook everything in the oven for about 50-60 minutes, stirring after every 15 minutes.
6. Remove everything from the heat and stir in the cranberries and keep aside to cool completely.
7. This granola can be stored in an airtight container.

ENGLISH STYLE
Scones

Prep Time: 20 mins
Total Time: 40 mins

Servings per Recipe: 8
Calories   311 kcal
Fat   13 g
Carbohydrates   42.1g
Protein   6.4 g
Cholesterol   48 mg
Sodium   243 mg

Ingredients

2 C. all-purpose flour
1/3 C. white sugar
1 tsp baking powder
1/2 tsp baking soda
1/4 tsp salt
6 tbsp shortening, chilled
2 apple - peeled, cored, and chopped
1 egg, lightly beaten
1/2 C. plain yogurt

1 tbsp milk
1 1/2 tsp almond extract
1 tbsp milk
1 egg, lightly beaten
2 tbsp cinnamon sugar
1/4 C. sliced almonds

Directions

1. Set your oven to 375 degrees F before doing anything else and line a baking sheet with parchment paper.
2. In a bowl, mix together the flour, baking soda, baking powder, sugar and salt.
3. With a pastry cutter, cut the shortening and mix till a coarse crumb mixture forms.
4. Fold in the chopped apples.
5. In another bowl, add the milk, yogurt, vanilla extract and 1 egg and beat till smooth.
6. Add the egg mixture into flour mixture and mix till well combined.
7. Place the dough onto a floured surface and knead for about 4-5 times.
8. Flat the dough into a 1 1/2-inch thick and 7-inch diameter circle and top with the almonds and cinnamon sugar evenly.

9. Cut dough into 8 wedges, and arrange on the prepared baking sheet.

10. In a small bowl, add the remaining egg and milk and beat well.

11. Coat the top of the scones with the milk mixture evenly and sprinkle with the almonds and cinnamon sugar.

12. Cook everything in the oven for about 20 minutes.

VALENTINE
Special Fudge

🥣 Prep Time: 10 mins

🕐 Total Time: 1 hr 20 mins

Servings per Recipe: 32

Calories	100 kcal
Fat	5.5 g
Carbohydrates	13.1g
Protein	0.9 g
Cholesterol	8 mg
Sodium	22 mg

Ingredients

3 C. confectioners' sugar
1/2 C. unsweetened cocoa powder
1/2 tsp ground cinnamon
1/2 C. butter
1/4 C. milk

1 1/2 tsp vanilla extract
1 C. chopped walnuts

Directions

1. Line an 8x8-inch baking dish with a greased foil paper.
2. In a bowl, mix together the cinnamon, cocoa and confectioners' sugar.
3. In a pan, heat the milk and butter on medium heat.
4. Stir in the vanilla extract.
5. Remove everything from the heat and immediately, stir in the walnuts.
6. Transfer the mixture into the prepared baking dish evenly.
7. Refrigerate for about 1 hour.
8. Carefully, remove the foil paper and cut the fudge into 2-inch squares and then cut each one in half diagonally.

Sweet Treat
Bars

Prep Time: 10 mins
Total Time: 40 mins

Servings per Recipe: 24
Calories	152 kcal
Fat	11.2 g
Carbohydrates	11.7g
Protein	1.8 g
Cholesterol	29 mg
Sodium	57 mg

Ingredients

1 C. butter, softened
1/4 C. white sugar
1 egg yolk
1 tsp vanilla extract
2 C. all-purpose flour
4 tsp ground cinnamon

1 egg white
1 C. chopped pecans
2 tbsp confectioners' sugar

Directions

1. Set your oven to 350 degrees F before doing anything else and grease a 13x9-inch baking dish.
2. In a bowl, add the sugar and butter and beat till creamy.
3. Add the egg yolks and vanilla extract and beat till smooth.
4. In another bowl, mix together the flour and cinnamon.
5. Add the sugar mixture and mix till well combined.
6. Transfer the mixture into the prepared baking dish evenly about 1/4-inch thickness.
7. Coat the top with the egg white evenly and sprinkle with the pecans, then press gently.
8. Cook everything in the oven for about 20-25 minutes.
9. Cut into the squares and serve with a sprinkling of the confectioners' sugar.

SIMPLY DELICIOUS
Oatmeal

Prep Time: 10 mins
Total Time: 55 mins

Servings per Recipe: 5

Calories	422 kcal
Fat	23.7 g
Carbohydrates	45.4g
Protein	10.5 g
Cholesterol	39 mg
Sodium	397 mg

Ingredients

2 C. rolled oats
1 C. unsweetened flaked coconut
1/4 C. light brown sugar
1 tsp baking powder
1 tsp ground cinnamon
1/2 tsp salt
2 C. skim milk

1 large egg, beaten
3 tbsp coconut oil, softened
1 tsp vanilla extract
1 1/2 C. blueberries

Directions

1. Set your oven to 350 degrees F before doing anything else and grease an 8-inch baking dish.
2. In a large bowl, mix together coconut, oats, baking powder, brown sugar, cinnamon and salt.
3. In another bowl, add remaining ingredients except blueberries and beat till well combined.
4. In the bottom of prepared baking dish, place about 2/3 of the blueberries evenly.
5. Place the oat mixture over the blueberries evenly and followed by egg mixture.
6. Top with the remaining blueberries evenly and cook everything in the oven for about 40 minutes.
7. Remove from oven and let it cool for about 5 minutes before serving.

Made in the USA
Coppell, TX
10 January 2022

71352030R10033